TABLE OF CONTENTS

INTRODUCTION

In the animal kingdom, the mother animal
usually cares for the young.
But some animal fathers do special things.
They make nests, and they sit on eggs.
They carry their young on their backs.

Some animal fathers take very special care
of their young.
They protect them and keep them close
to the nest.
They show their children where to find food,
water, and shelter.

PATIENT PAPAS
Emperor Penguins

Emperor penguins are
the largest of all penguins.
They spend a lot of time
in the water.
On land they hop, jump,
and run.
Sometimes they slide
on their stomachs.

Emperor penguins can't fly,
but they have feathers
and really are birds.

They live near the South Pole,
where it is very cold.
They have two layers of feathers.
Their stiff outer feathers
keep them dry.
Their soft inner feathers
help to keep them warm.

Emperor penguin fathers
do something special.
After the mother lays an egg,
the father penguin takes over.
He holds the egg on his feet,
and covers it with a flap of skin.
Then he waits and waits.

When it storms, he and the other
father penguins stand together.
The father eats nothing but snow
for almost three months.
He loses a lot of weight.
After the baby penguin hatches,
the father can go get lunch!

SWIFT SIRES
Ostriches, Emus, and Cassowaries

Ostriches, emus, and cassowaries
are all ratites.
This means that they can't fly,
even though they have wings.

Ostriches live in Africa.
They are the largest living bird
in the world.
Adult males can be eight feet tall.
Ostriches can run very fast –
up to forty miles per hour.
They also live a very long time –
up to seventy years.

Emus live in Australia.
Emus can be up to six feet tall.
They are the second largest bird
in the world.
Like ostriches, emus have
very long legs and can run fast.

Ostrich father with eggs and chicks

Emu father with chicks

9

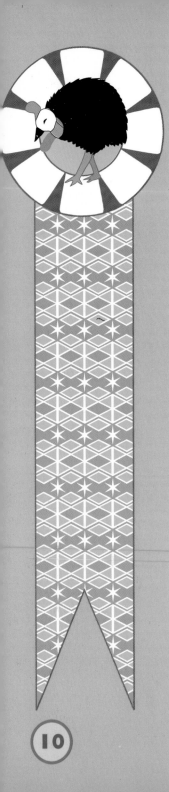

Cassowaries live in Australia
and New Guinea.
They are almost as tall as emus.
They have bright blue heads
with a crest that helps them
to break through undergrowth.
They can move very quickly.

Cassowary

Ostrich, emu, and cassowary fathers
do something special.
After the mothers lay their eggs,
the fathers and mothers take turns
sitting on the nest to warm the eggs.
The father often does all of the nest-sitting.

After the chicks are born,
the father looks after the children.
He warns them of danger and helps them
to find food, water, and shelter.

Emu

Cassowary

HOPPING POPS
Arrow-Poison Frogs

Arrow-poison frogs are beautiful.
They look like painted pebbles,
and brighten up the rain forests
of Central and South America.
Their colorful bodies tell us,
"Beware! Don't eat me.
I'm poisonous!"

In fact, one of the most deadly
poisons made by any animal comes
from the skins of these small frogs.
Hunters use the poison
on darts and arrows.
One tiny frog carries
enough poison for forty arrows.

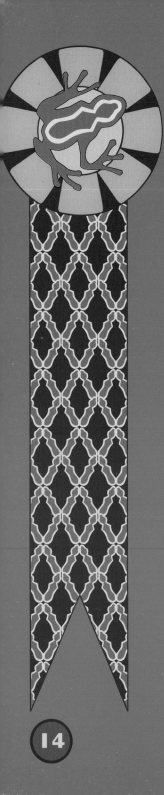

The father arrow-poison frog does
something special.
First he sings a humming,
chirping song as the mother frog
lays her eggs.
She usually lays six.

Most frogs lay eggs in water,
but arrow-poison frogs lay
their eggs on land on a leaf.
The father frog stands guard
until the eggs hatch.

After hatching, the tiny tadpoles
wiggle up onto their father's back.
He then hops with his babies
to a new home in a safe puddle.
Soon the tadpoles
will become beautiful,
but dangerous, frogs.

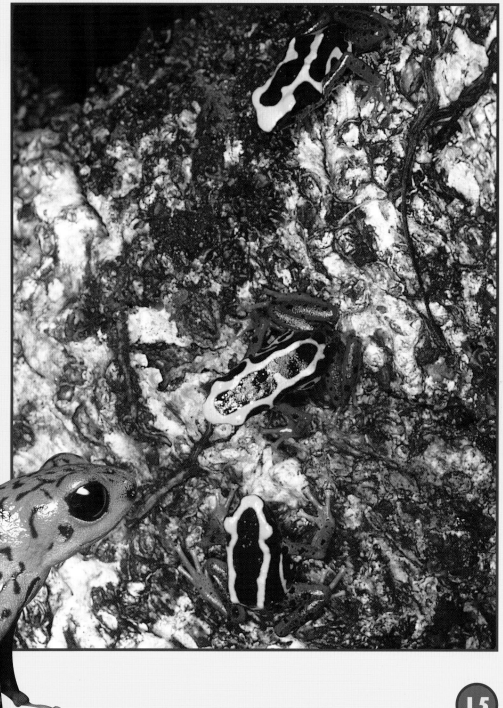

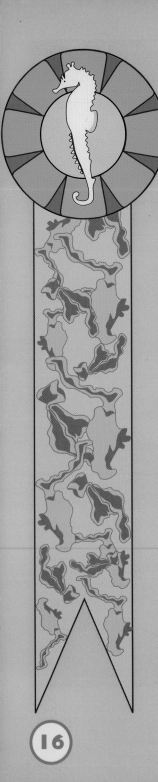

FISHY FATHERS
Seahorses and Sticklebacks

You can't saddle up a seahorse.
Seahorses aren't horses at all.
They are small fish.
A seahorse's body is made
of bony plates.
Seahorses don't have
many enemies.
Maybe they are too crunchy!

Seahorses can't swim very well.
They use their tails to hold on
to ocean plants.
Seahorses can change colors
to blend in with the plants.
When their food swims by,
they suck it into their mouths.

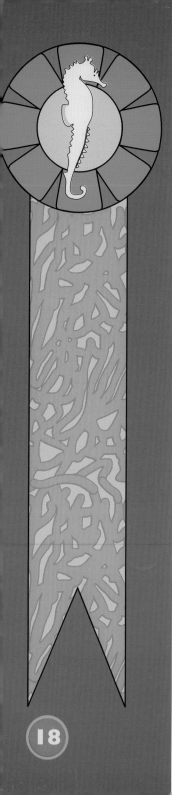

Father seahorses
do something special.
They have pouches
in their stomachs.
After the mother lays eggs
in the father's pouch, she leaves.

The father carries his growing
family for up to forty-five days.
His babies get so big
that he can barely swim.
At last his pouch pops open
and out pour the little seahorses.
They look like small commas.

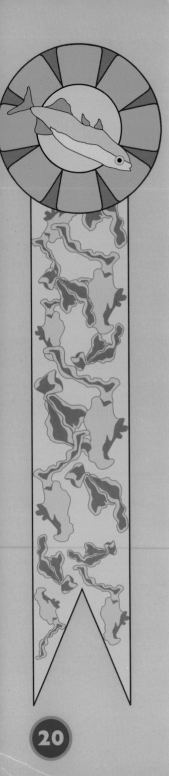

Sticklebacks are tiny fish.
The stickleback is usually
a bluish silver color,
but at nesting time,
the male's belly turns
a bright orange red.

A stickleback father does
something special.
He gathers algae and shapes it
into a small, tube-shaped nest.
Then he does a dance to guide
the mother into the nest,
where she lays her eggs.

The father watches over the eggs until they hatch.
He doesn't leave, even to eat!

The father watches over the baby fish for several days.
If one wanders off, he sucks it into his mouth
and spits it back into the nest.

SWINGING DADS
Gibbons and Tamarins

Gibbons live in the jungles
of Southeast Asia,
and are the smallest of all apes.
They use their long arms
to swing through the trees.

Tamarins are monkeys
that live in the rain forests
of Central and South America.
They are smaller than gibbons,
but they have long tails.
They use their arms and tails
to swing from tree to tree.

Tamarin

Gibbon and tamarin fathers do something special.
The fathers often carry around their young
as they move among the treetops.
A gibbon father carries his young on his hip.
A tamarin father carries his young on his back,
where they cling tightly to his long fur
as he swings along high above the ground.
What a ride!

Gibbon

INDEX

Words for Father in Other Languages

Albanian – Baba

Chinese – Fù

Dutch – Vader

Finnish – Isä

French – Père

German – Vater

Italian – Padre

Malayan – Ayah

Norwegian – Far

Portuguese – Pai

Vietnamese – Cha

Welsh – Tad